HEROES OF BLACK HISTORY

OPRAH WINFREY

BY JANEY LEVY

Gareth Stevens PUBLISHING

Please visit our website, www.garethstevens.com. For a free color catalog of all our high-quality books, call toll free 1-800-542-2595 or fax 1-877-542-2596.

Library of Congress Cataloging-in-Publication Data
Names: Levy, Janey, author.
Title: Oprah Winfrey / Janey Levy.
Description: New York : Gareth Stevens Publishing, [2021] | Series: Heroes of black history | Includes index. | Contents: Meet Oprah Winfrey – A hard childhood – Turning her life around – Starting her career – Finding fame – New adventures – What's next?
Identifiers: LCCN 2019051298 | ISBN 9781538258125 (library binding) | ISBN 9781538258101 (paperback) | ISBN 9781538258118 (6 Pack) | ISBN 9781538258132 (ebook)
Subjects: LCSH: Winfrey, Oprah–Juvenile literature. | Television personalities–United States–Biography–Juvenile literature. | Actors–United States–Biography–Juvenile literature.
Classification: LCC PN1992.4.W56 L46 2021 | DDC 791.4502/8092 [B]–dc23
LC record available at https://lccn.loc.gov/2019051298

First Edition

Published in 2021 by
Gareth Stevens Publishing
111 East 14th Street, Suite 349
New York, NY 10003

Designer: Laura Bowen
Editor: Monika Davies

Photo credits: Cover, p. 1 (Oprah Winfrey) Vera Anderson/Contributor/WireImage/Getty Images; cover, p. 1 (background) Gregreesehd/Wikimedia Commons; p. 5 J. Countess/Contributor/Getty Images Europe/Getty Images; p. 7 Chillin662/Wikimedia Commons; p. 9 Adriane Jaeckle/Stringer/Getty Images North America/Getty Images; p. 11 Sean Pavone/Shutterstock.com; p. 13 Kaldari/Wikimedia Commons; p. 15 Afro Newspaper/Gado/Contributor/Archive Photos/Getty Images; p. 17 (Baltimore) f11photo/Shutterstock.com; p. 17 (map) Ad_hominem/Shutterstock.com; p. 19 Ron Galella/Contributor/Ron Galella Collection/Getty Images; p. 21 (top) Archive Photos/Stringer/Moviepix/Getty Images; p. 21 (bottom) Sunset Boulevard/Contributor/Corbis Historical/Getty Images; p. 23 Getty Images/Handout/Hulton Archive/Getty Images; p. 25 Getty Images/Staff/Getty Images North America/Getty Images; p. 27 Rena Schild/Shutterstock.com.

Printed in the United States of America

CPSIA compliance information: Batch #CS20GS: For further information contact Gareth Stevens, New York, New York at 1-800-542-2595.

CONTENTS

Words in the glossary appear in **bold** type the first time they are used in the text.

MEET OPRAH WINFREY

You may have heard of Oprah Winfrey. She's one of the richest and most **influential** women in the United States. But how much do you really know about her?

Oprah was born into **poverty** and endured suffering as a child. But she turned her life around with her father's help. She started her career anchoring, or leading, newscasts on television, but she soon was leading her own television talk shows. Oprah then went on to become an actor and establish a magazine. She also started her own companies to make television shows and movies. Inside this book, you'll learn more about Oprah, a truly **progressive** leader.

WHAT'S A TALK SHOW?

A talk show is a program where the host, who's usually a well-known individual, **interviews** famous people and other guests. There are different kinds of talk shows. Some talk shows aim to entertain their viewers. Others deal with political or social issues. Other talk shows may address emotional concerns.

Time magazine has celebrated Oprah as the "first woman to own and produce her own talk show."

A HARD CHILDHOOD

Oprah Gail Winfrey was born January 29, 1954, on a small farm in Kosciusko, Mississippi. Her mother was Vernita Lee, and her father was Vernon Winfrey. Her parents separated soon after she was born, and her mother moved north to find work. Young Oprah stayed with her grandmother on the farm.

Life on the farm was simple, and Oprah didn't have much as a child. But she had the love and encouragement of her grandmother and her church community. Her grandmother taught her to read when she was only 3 years old.

WHAT CAN A KID DO FOR FUN?

What did young Oprah do for fun on her grandmother's farm? Sometimes she told stories to a crowd of farm animals. She also had a favorite doll made out of a corncob. Church also was an important part of Oprah's life. By the time she was 3, she was reading poems and Bible verses out loud at church.

Kosciusko, Mississippi, is a small town. The year Oprah was born, fewer than 6,800 people lived there.

A dark period in young Oprah's life began when she was 6. This is when she went to live with her mother in Milwaukee, Wisconsin. The neighborhood where her mother lived was poor and dangerous.

Oprah's mother worked as a maid and was gone during the day. Men mistreated and abused Oprah while her mother was away. This lasted from when she was 9 until she was 13. And, she had no one to tell about these experiences. Oprah tried to run away to escape. She later said, "I started acting out my need for attention, my need to be loved."

BIG CHANGES FOR A LITTLE GIRL

Try to imagine how the huge changes in her life would have made young Oprah feel. She went from a small farm to a big city. She also went from being with her grandmother all day to being left alone while her mother worked. She went from a loving home to a place where she was abused and mistreated.

Oprah briefly lived with her father in Nashville, Tennessee, around two years after she first moved to Milwaukee. She returned to live with her mother when she was 9 years old.

TURNING HER LIFE AROUND

Oprah's life took a turn for the better when her mother sent her to live with her father in Nashville. Oprah was a headstrong 14-year-old when she arrived at her father's home. Her father was very strict, or firm, with her. After years of acting out, this proved to be just what Oprah needed.

Oprah's father provided her with a safe, secure home life. She had structure and rules. She had to meet a **curfew**. Every two weeks, he required her to read three books and write book reports on each one. She had to learn five new words each day—or no dinner!

WHAT OPRAH SAYS

Oprah spoke about what it was like living with her tough father. She said, "As strict as he was, he... would not accept anything less than what he thought was my best." She's also said, "[My father] saved me. He simply knew what he wanted and expected. He would take nothing less."

When young Oprah moved to Nashville, the city's population was almost 700,000.

Under her father's care, Oprah flourished. She became an honor student, joined the drama club, and served on the student council. She won prizes for public speaking and **dramatic** readings. In one speaking contest, Oprah won a full **scholarship** to Tennessee State University. She also was invited to a White House Conference on Youth.

A radio station for Nashville's black community then hired her to read the news reports in the afternoon. In her first year of college, Oprah won the Miss Black Nashville and Miss Black Tennessee beauty contests. The young girl from a Mississippi farm had come a long way.

ABOUT TENNESSEE STATE UNIVERSITY

Tennessee State University is one of many historically black colleges and universities in the country. These were established to provide higher education for black people at a time when they weren't allowed to go to other colleges and universities. The university is located in Nashville and had a student population of around 8,000 in 2018.

Oprah began working towards a degree in Mass Communication at Tennessee State University.

STARTING HER CAREER

When Oprah was 19, she began working for her local CBS television station as a **news anchor**. She originally turned down the job twice. After all, she was just in her second year of college. But one of her teachers convinced her to accept it, pointing out that working at CBS was why "people [went] to college."

After Oprah graduated in 1976, she moved to Baltimore, Maryland, for a new job at an ABC news station. There, she was both a **reporter** and a news anchor. However, that job didn't last long. As a reporter, Oprah was supposed to be objective, which didn't suit her nature.

IN OPRAH'S WORDS

Speaking about being a news anchor, Oprah said, "I always felt like I had a pretend voice when I went on the air. I would interview people who'd been through [horrible events], and . . . I would **empathize**, and then I would get written up by my bosses."

As a news anchor, Oprah said, "I never felt comfortable in my own skin. It never felt authentic [sincere] to me."

In 1977, Oprah's bosses moved her to a morning talk show called *People Are Talking*. She immediately felt at home on this show. She could ask exactly the questions she wanted to ask, and she could empathize with her guests.

In January 1984, Oprah moved to Chicago, Illinois, to take over a half-hour talk show called *AM Chicago*. The show was always last in the ratings. But Oprah changed the kind of topics the show covered. This new selection of topics, along with Oprah's caring personality, made the show popular. In September 1985, the show grew to an hour long and was renamed *The Oprah Winfrey Show*. She'd later describe her show as "hour-long life lessons."

OPRAH ON HER FIRST TALK SHOW

"It wouldn't have mattered who the guests were, because when I. . .could ask questions just based upon what I wanted to know. . .it felt like coming home. When that first show ended, on August 14, 1978, I said, 'I have found my home. This is what I was meant to do.'"

IMPORTANT PLACES IN OPRAH'S LIFE

This map shows important places in Oprah's life, including where she was born, where she lived with her mother, where she grew up with her father, where she had her first talk show, and where she had the job that made her famous.

FINDING FAME

Oprah enjoyed great fame in Chicago by the end of 1985. But her fame was about to grow immensely. In 1986, *The Oprah Winfrey Show* began to be shown in cities across the country. It soon became the number one talk show in America.

In 1987, the show received three daytime Emmys. The Television Academy hands out Emmys to honor accomplishments in television programming. *The Oprah Winfrey Show* won for best talk show, best talk show host, and best direction in a talk show. The next year, Oprah became the first black woman to receive the International Radio and Television Society's Broadcaster of the Year Award.

MORE AWARDS

Oprah continued to receive honor after honor. In 1986, the Chicago Academy for the Arts gave her an award for her unique, or special, contributions to Chicago's arts community. The same year, the National Organization of Women named her a Woman of Achievement.

This photograph shows Oprah with one of her Emmys at the 14th annual Daytime Emmy Awards in 1987.

In 1985, Oprah found further fame as an actor. She was one of the stars of *The Color Purple*, a movie based on Alice Walker's award-winning book of the same name. Oprah's performance in the movie was so good that she was nominated, or suggested, for two awards for best supporting actress: an Oscar and a Golden Globe Award.

Oprah starred in another movie in 1986. *Native Son* was based on a book written by Richard Wright. Once again, Oprah earned praise for her performance. The young woman who failed as a news anchor had now found success as a talk show host and actor.

THE COLOR PURPLE

The Color Purple tells the story of a young black woman in the South who is trying to figure out who she is after decades of abuse from the men in her life. She finds healing at the end. Alice Walker's 1982 novel is considered an inspiring story and was praised by many upon publication.

These photographs from *The Color Purple* show Oprah as Sofia, a tough, or unbending, character.

NEW ADVENTURES

You might think Oprah's talk show and acting would leave her with little time or energy for anything else. But Oprah had much more that she wanted to accomplish. In 1986, Oprah put together her own television production company, Harpo Productions. Her company produced television shows about subjects she thought were important. Her company was behind the TV miniseries *The Women of Brewster Place* in 1989. Oprah was one of the show's stars.

In 1990, Oprah formed Harpo Films, a movie production company. It produced *Before Women Had Wings* in 1997, as well as Toni Morrison's *Beloved* in 1998. Oprah starred in both.

STARRING OPRAH'S VOICE

Oprah's acting career isn't limited to dramatic films. She's also given her voice to characters in many animated, or cartoon, movies over the years. Her animated film list includes *Charlotte's Web* (2006), *Bee Movie* (2007), *The Princess and the Frog* (2009), and *The Star* (2017).

This shows Oprah filming the movie *Beloved*, produced by her production company Harpo Films. What do you get if you spell "Harpo" backward?

Meanwhile, Oprah was still running *The Oprah Winfrey Show.* In 1996, she started an on-air book club. She said she wanted "to get the country reading." She chose a book and told her viewers to buy it. The book would then be talked about on her show the next month. Each book she chose quickly became a **best seller**.

Still looking for ways to put subjects she thought were important on television, Oprah became one of the founders of Oxygen Media in 1998. It's a cable channel that shows programs mostly for women. Oprah also got into publishing. In 2000, she began publishing the successful *O, the Oprah Magazine.*

BEGINNINGS AND ENDINGS

Big changes happened for Oprah in 2011. She created the Oprah Winfrey Network (OWN), which replaced the Discovery Health Channel. She ended *The Oprah Winfrey Show* after 25 years, but she didn't leave television. In 2012, she started a weekly evening interview program called *Oprah's Next Chapter.* It appears on OWN.

All of Oprah's businesses helped to make her very wealthy. By 2003, she was a billionaire—the first black woman to become one.

Oprah is also a philanthropist, or someone who gives money and their time to help improve the lives of others. She created Oprah's Angel Network, which supports charitable projects around the world. In 2007, she opened the Oprah Winfrey Leadership Academy for Girls in South Africa. She also gave more than $20 million to the National Museum of African American History and Culture in Washington, DC.

Oprah has received awards for her philanthropic work. The Academy of Motion Picture Arts and Sciences gave her the Jean Hersholt **Humanitarian** Award in 2011. And in 2013, President Obama awarded her the Presidential Medal of Freedom.

FIGHTING ABUSE

As she'd experienced abuse as a young girl, Oprah wanted to help protect children from child abusers. She began a campaign to establish a national database of people guilty of child abuse. She spoke before a Senate committee in support of a bill that would establish the database. The "Oprah Bill" was signed into law in 1993.

The Presidential Medal of Freedom is the highest honor given to someone who's not in the military.

WHAT'S NEXT?

What's next for this energetic woman? Oprah is certainly not slowing down. She's launched a new global book club as part of a partnership with Apple and has upcoming speaking tours.

After a speech Oprah gave at the 2018 Golden Globes Awards, there was even talk she might run for president. The emotional, spirited speech was a call for equality for everyone. Many thought it was a powerful speech and it might mean she was thinking of running for president. But Oprah has said publicly she's not interested in running for president. And yet... who knows what the future might hold for this remarkable woman?

A POWERFUL WOMAN

Oprah has been said to be the richest African American of the 20th century. Her name is on every list of important opinion-makers. Some consider her to be "the most powerful woman in the world." That's pretty amazing when you think that there are many important women political leaders around the world!

A TIMELINE OF OPRAH'S LIFE

JANUARY 29, 1954	Oprah is born in Kosciusko, Mississippi.
1960	Oprah moves to Milwaukee, Wisconsin, to live with her mother.
1968	Oprah goes to live with father in Nashville, Tennessee.
1973	Oprah becomes a news anchor for the Nashville CBS TV station.
1977	Oprah becomes host of *People Are Talking* in Baltimore.
1984	Oprah moves to Chicago to host *AM Chicago.*
1985	*AM Chicago* is renamed *The Oprah Winfrey Show,* and Oprah stars in *The Color Purple.*
1986	*The Oprah Winfrey Show* becomes a national show, and Oprah founds television production company, Harpo Productions.
1996	Oprah founds her on-air book club.
1998	Oprah stars in *Beloved* and helps found Oxygen Media.
2000	Oprah begins publishing *O, the Oprah Magazine.*
2011	Oprah ends *The Oprah Winfrey Show* and creates the OWN network.
2013	Oprah receives the Presidential Medal of Freedom.
2020	Oprah goes on a cross-country speaking tour.

GLOSSARY

abuse: a misuse of power, such as the harmful treatment of a person, that is often illegal

best seller: a popular item that a great number of people have purchased

curfew: the time set by a caretaker at which a young person has to return home

dramatic: greatly affecting people in an emotional way

empathize: to feel the same emotions or feelings as another person

humanitarian: having to do with working for the health and happiness of other people

influential: having an effect on

interview: to question or talk with someone to learn more about them and their story

news anchor: someone who reads the news on a television show

poverty: the state of being poor and not having enough money to meet basic needs

progressive: supporting and interested in modern ideas especially in regards to politics and education

reporter: someone who tells people the news and gives information on television

scholarship: money awarded to a student to pay for their college education

FOR MORE INFORMATION

BOOKS

Dakers, Diane. *Oprah Winfrey: Media Legend and Inspiration to Millions.* New York, NY: Crabtree Publishing, 2016.

Kramer, Barbara. *Who Is Oprah Winfrey?* New York, NY: Penguin Workshop, 2019.

Moss, Caroline. *Work It, Girl: Oprah Winfrey: Run the Show Like CEO.* London, UK: Frances Lincoln Children's Books, 2019.

WEBSITES

Oprah Winfrey
time.com/collection/firsts/4898535/oprah-winfrey-firsts
Watch a short interview with Oprah about starting her own talk show.

Oprah Winfrey Fast Facts
edition.cnn.com/2013/08/05/us/oprah-winfrey-fast-facts/index.html
Follow a timeline of Oprah's life here.

Oprah Winfrey's Official Biography
www.oprah.com/pressroom/oprah-winfreys-official-biography
Learn more about Oprah's life story on her website.

Publisher's note to educators and parents: Our editors have carefully reviewed these websites to ensure that they are suitable for students. Many websites change frequently, however, and we cannot guarantee that a site's future contents will continue to meet our high standards of quality and educational value. Be advised that students should be closely supervised whenever they access the internet.

INDEX